Keys to Understanding

Faith

Dr. Jerry Falwell

Introduction

You hold in your hand a book that is intended to assist you in your time of daily devotional and prayer. Daily life is woven together with the threads of habit, and no habit is more important to your spiritual growth than the discipline of daily prayer and devotion to God. This text is intended to help. It is divided into 30 chapters, one for each day of the month. Each chapter contains Bible verses, quotations from notable Christian thinkers, a brief essay, a prayer, and lots of space for you to make notes. Every chapter deals with a differing aspect of a vitally important Biblical theme: The Power of Faith.

During the next 30 days, please try this experiment: Read one chapter each day. If you're already committed to a daily worship time, this book will enrich that experience. If you are not, the simple act of giving God a few minutes each morning will change the tone and direction of your life. When you give time to God each day, God will bless you, and then you, in turn, can share His saving message with a world that desperately needs His healing touch. May you trust God always, and may He richly bless you and yours.

Jerry Falwell

Contents

Day 1: The Power of Faith...13
Day 2: Faith in God's Miracles.......................................17
Day 3: Faith for Today..21
Day 4: Faith in Times of Discouragement.....................25
Day 5: Faith in Times of Suffering................................29
Day 6: Faith in the Power of Prayer..............................33
Day 7: Faith in God's Timing...37
Day 8: Faith and Renewal..41
Day 9: Faith in God, Not in Oneself.............................45
Day 10: Faith in Adversity...49
Day 11: Faith and Obedience..53
Day 12: Materialism: The Spiritual Roadblock............57
Day 13: Sharing Your Faith..61
Day 14: Faith in the Father..65
Day 15: Faith Without Fear...69
Day 16: Faith in Quiet Moments...................................73
Day 17: Faith in Our Salvation......................................77
Day 18: Faith Beyond the Crowd..................................81
Day 19: Born Again Faith...85
Day 20: Have Faith . . . And Get Busy...........................89
Day 21: Faith Beyond Understanding...........................93
Day 22: Faith in the Dark..97
Day 23: A Perfect Faith for Imperfect People.............101
Day 24: Faith in God's Word.......................................105
Day 25: Faith in the Presence of God.........................109
Day 26: Faith in Times of Prosperity..........................113
Day 27: Faith for a Loved One's Conversion...............117
Day 28: Faith in the Promises of Jesus.......................121
Day 29: Faith Beyond the Grave..................................125
Day 30: Faith in God..129

Sunday Note..133

Selected Bible Verses...145

Day 1

The Power of Faith

But Jesus turned around, and when He saw her,
He said, "Be of good cheer, daughter,
your faith has made you well."
And the woman was made well from that hour.

Matthew 9:22

The familiar story from the book of Matthew gives us hope. A suffering woman sought healing by simply touching the hem of Jesus' garment. When she did so, Christ turned to her and said, "Be of good cheer, daughter, your faith has made you well" (9:22). We, too, can be made whole when we place our faith completely and unwaveringly in the person of Jesus Christ.

If your faith is being tested to the point of breaking, remember that Your Savior is near. When you reach out to Him in faith, He will give you peace, assurance, and spiritual abundance. If you are content to touch even the smallest fragment of the Master's garment, He will make you whole— not only for this instant and not only for this day— but for all eternity.

Faith reposes on the character of God,
and if we believe that God is perfect, we must
conclude that his ways are perfect also.

A. W. Tozer

The measure of faith must always determine
the measure of power and of blessing.
Faith can only live by feeding on
what is Divine, on God Himself.

Andrew Murray

Little faith will bring your soul to heaven;
great faith will bring heaven to your soul.

C. H. Spurgeon

Be of good courage, and He shall strengthen
your heart, all you who hope in the LORD.

Psalm 31:24

A Prayer

Dear Lord, make me Your obedient,
faithful servant. You are with me always.
Strengthen my faith in You, Father,
and let me remember that with Your love
and Your power, I can live courageously
and victoriously today and every day.
Amen

Notes:_____

_____

_____

_____

_____

_____

_____

_____

_____

_____

_____

_____

Day 2

Faith in God's Miracles

But Jesus looked at them and said,
"With men it is impossible, but not with God;
for with God all things are possible."

Mark 10:27

Do you believe in God's miraculous provision? You should. But perhaps, as you have faced the inevitable struggles of life, you have—without realizing it—placed limitations upon God. To do so is a profound mistake. God's power has no limitations, and God can work mighty miracles in your own life *if* you let Him.

Do you lack the faith that God can do miraculous things in your life or the lives of your loved ones? If so, it's time to reconsider. Are you a "Doubting Thomas," or a "Negative Nancy"? If so, you are attempting to place limitations on a God who has none. Instead of doubting Him, you must trust in God. Instead of doubting His power, you must trust it. When you do, God will change your life today, tomorrow, *and* forever, Amen.

Too many Christians live below the miracle level.
Vance Havner

When God is involved, anything can happen.
Be open and stay that way. God has a beautiful
way of bringing good vibrations out
of broken chords.
Charles Swindoll

Power with God is the highest attainment
of the life of full abiding.
Andrew Murray

You are the God who does wonders;
You have declared Your strength
among the peoples.
Psalm 77:14

A Prayer

Dear Lord, absolutely nothing is impossible
for You. Let me trust in Your power and in
Your miracles. When I lose hope, give me faith;
when others lose hope, let me tell them of
Your glorious works. Today, Lord, keep me mindful
that You are a God of infinite possibilities
and infinite love.

Amen

Notes:_____

_____

_____

_____

_____

_____

_____

_____

_____

_____

_____

_____

_____

Day 3

Faith for Today

This is the day the LORD has made;
we will rejoice and be glad in it.

Psalm 118:24

What do you expect from the day ahead? Are you expecting God to do wonderful things, or are you living beneath a cloud of apprehension and doubt? The familiar words of Psalm 118:24 remind us of a profound yet simple truth: *"This is the day the LORD has made; we will rejoice and be glad in it."*

For Christian believers, every day begins and ends with God and His Son. Christ came to this earth to give us abundant life and eternal salvation. We give thanks to our Maker when we treasure each day and use it to the fullest. Today, let's give thanks for this day and for the One who created it. And then, let's use this day—a precious gift from the Father above—to serve our Savior and to share His Good News with all who cross our paths.

A man can no more take in a supply of grace
for the future than he can eat enough for
the next six months, or take sufficient air into
his lungs at one time to sustain life for a week.
We must draw upon God's boundless store of
grace from day to day as we need it.

D. L. Moody

Now is the only time worth having because,
indeed, it is the only time we have.

C. H. Spurgeon

Each day, each moment is so pregnant with
eternity that if we "tune in" to it,
we can hardly contain the joy.

Gloria Gaither

Thanks be to God for His indescribable gift!

2 Corinthians 9:15

A Prayer

Dear Lord, You have given me another day
of life. Let me celebrate this day, and let me use it
according to Your plan. I come to You today with
faith in my heart and praise on my lips. I praise
You, Father, for the gift of life and for the friends
and family members who make my life rich.
Enable me to live each moment to the fullest,
totally involved in Your will.
Amen

Notes:_____

_____

_____

_____

_____

_____

_____

_____

_____

_____

_____

_____

_____

Day 4

Faith in Times of Discouragement

I called on the Lord in distress;
The LORD answered me and set me
in a broad place. The LORD is on my side;
I will not fear. What can man do to me?

Psalm 118:5, 6

Faith and discouragement are opposites. Faith is taking God at His Word no matter how bleak the circumstances may appear. Discouragement, on the other hand, is focusing on distressing circumstances in spite of what God has promised.

Learn to trust God. Believe when you cannot see, hear, or feel. Then, you will know you are pleasing God *and* you will allow God to do wonderful things in you and through you.

Working in the vineyard, working all the day,
Never be discouraged, only watch and pray.
Fanny Crosby

Discouraged people, if they must be discouraged,
ought, at least, to keep their discouragements to
themselves, hidden away in the privacy of their
own bosoms lest they should discourage
the hearts of their brethren.
Hannah Whitall Smith

Don't take tomorrow to bed with you.
Norman Vincent Peale

But seek first the kingdom of God and
His righteousness, and all these things
shall be added to you. Therefore
do not worry about tomorrow, for
tomorrow will worry about its own things.
Sufficient for the day is its own trouble.
Matthew 6:33, 34

A Prayer

Dear Lord, when I am discouraged, give me
perspective and faith. When I am weak,
give me strength. When I am fearful,
give me courage for the day ahead. I will trust
in Your promises, Father, and I will live with
the assurance that You are with me not only
for this day, but also throughout all eternity.
Amen

Notes:_____

_____

_____

_____

_____

_____

_____

_____

_____

_____

_____

_____

_____

_____

Day 5

Faith in Times of Suffering

I have heard your prayer, I have seen your tears;
surely, I will heal you.

2 Kings 20:5

Do you feel like God is punishing you? In some Christian circles, the leaders teach that when you are in God's will, no tragedy can ever strike you. They believe that somewhere in the Bible it says if you win souls, if you give to the church, if you pray and read the Scriptures, then you will never encounter obstacles to the happiness and success you desire. But such a doctrine is false!

When we examine the lives of the disciples of Jesus after His ascension, we see that these men were imprisoned, beaten, even killed. Yet no one would say that these martyrs were living outside of God's will, and no one should ever doubt their Christianity.

God promises us eternal life through His Son Jesus Christ, but God does not promise us that our earthly lives will be free from suffering. Instead, He promises that He will give strength to the weary and healing to those who grieve. God promises that wherever we are, whether at the peak of the mountaintop or in the darkness of the deepest valley, He will be with us always . . . and that promise, dear friends, is always enough.

Suffering is no argument of God's displeasure;
it is simply a part of the fiber of our lives.
Fanny Crosby

When all else is gone, God is still left.
Nothing changes Him.
Hannah Whitall Smith

God of our life, there are days when the burdens
we carry chafe our shoulders and weigh us down;
when the road seems dreary and endless, when
our lives have no music in them, and our hearts
are lonely, and our souls have lost their courage.
Flood the path with light, run our eyes to where
the skies are full of promise; tune our hearts to
brave music; and so quicken our spirits that we
may be able to encourage the souls of all who
journey with us on the road of life,
to Your honor and glory.
St. Augustine

The LORD gives you rest from your sorrow,
and from your fear....
Isaiah 14:3

A Prayer

Dear Lord, Your Word promises that You will
not give us more than we can bear; You have
promised to give us rest from our sorrows and
deliverance from our pain. Today, Father, I pray
for those who suffer and for those who mourn.
And I thank You for sustaining us in our days
of sorrow. May we trust You always
and praise You forever.
Amen

Notes:_____

_____

_____

_____

_____

_____

_____

_____

_____

_____

_____

Day 6

Faith in the Power of Prayer

The effective, fervent prayer of a righteous man
avails much.

James 5:16

There are some things money will do; there are some things human effort will do; there are some things that human ingenuity will do; but there are some things that only God can do. And He will not do them until someone prays.

Are you a prayer warrior, or have you retreated from God's battlefield? Do you pray about almost everything or about almost nothing? Do you pray only at mealtimes, or do you pray at all times? The answer to these questions will determine, to a surprising extent, the degree to which God will use you for the glory of His kingdom.

God promises that the prayers of righteous men and women can accomplish great things. So pray. Start praying before the sun comes up and keep praying until you fall off to sleep at night. And rest assured: God is always listening and He always wants to hear from you.

Prayer succeeds when all else fails.
E. M. Bounds

To pray in the name of Jesus is not only to use
His name at the end of a prayer, but it is to pray
in the mind and in the spirit of Jesus.
R. A. Torrey

If you lack knowledge, go to school.
If you lack wisdom, get on your knees.
Vance Havner

Watch therefore, and pray always....
Luke 21:36

A Prayer

Dear Lord, make me a person whose constant
prayers are pleasing to You. Let me come to You
often with concerns both great and small.
I trust in the power of prayer, Father, because
prayer changes things *and* it changes me.
In the quiet moments of the day, I will open
my heart to You. I know that You are with
me always and that You always hear my prayers.
So I will pray and be thankful.
Amen

Notes:_____

_____

_____

_____

_____

_____

_____

_____

_____

_____

_____

_____

_____

_____

Day 7

Faith in God's Timing

Therefore humble yourselves under the mighty
hand of God, that he may exalt you in due time.

1 Peter 5:6

Sometimes, because we are impatient, hardheaded human beings, the hardest thing to do is to wait. This is especially true when we're in a hurry and when we want things to happen now, if not sooner! But God's plan does not always happen in the way that we would like or at the time of our own choosing. Our task—as believing Christians who trust in a benevolent, all knowing Father—is to wait patiently for God to reveal Himself.

We mortals are, by nature, an impatient lot. We know what we want, and we know exactly when we want it: RIGHT NOW! But, God knows better. He has created a world that unfolds according to His own timetable, not ours . . . thank goodness!

He whose attitude towards Christ is correct does indeed ask "in His Name" and receives what he asks for if it is something which does not stand in the way of his salvation. He gets it, however, only when he ought to receive it, for certain things are not refused us, but their granting is delayed to a fitting time.

St. Augustine

Grass that is here today and gone tomorrow does not require much time to mature. A big oak tree that lasts for generations requires much more time to grow and mature. God is concerned about your life through eternity. Allow Him to take all the time He needs to shape you for His purposes. Larger assignments will require longer periods of preparation.

Henry Blackaby

For you have need of endurance, so that after you have done the will of God, you may receive the promise.

Hebrews 10:36

A Prayer

Heavenly Father, give me patience. Let me live according to Your plan and according to Your timetable. When I am hurried, slow me down. When I become impatient with others, give me empathy. When I am frustrated by the demands of the day, give me peace. Today, let me be a patient Christian, Dear Lord, as I trust in You and in Your master plan for my life.

Amen

Notes:_____

_____

_____

_____

_____

_____

_____

_____

_____

_____

_____

_____

_____

_____

_____

Day 8

Faith and Renewal

I will give you a new heart
and put a new spirit within you....

Ezekiel 36:26

God will never place more burdens upon you than He knows you can bear. And at the moment when you think that you have trusted God all you can, when you have prayed all you that know how to pray, when you have cried your last tear and sighed your last sigh, then, at that very moment, God will take you into Elim and renew your life.

Are you tired or troubled? Turn your heart toward God in prayer. Are you weak or worried? Make the time to delve deeply into God's Holy Word. When you do, you'll discover that the Creator of the universe stands ready and able to create a new sense of wonderment and joy in you.

The same voice that brought Lazarus out
of the tomb raised us to newness of life.
C. H. Spurgeon

Oh, the tranquil joy of that dear retreat,
where the Savior bids thee rest,
With steadfast hope, and a trusting faith,
In His love secure and blest.
Fanny Crosby

Father, for this day, renew within me
the gift of the Holy Spirit.
Andrew Murray

He makes me to lie down in green pastures;
He leads me beside the still waters.
He restores my soul.
Psalm 23:2, 3

A Prayer

Dear Lord, sometimes I grow weary; sometimes
I am discouraged; sometimes I am fearful.
Yet when I turn my heart and my prayers to You,
I am secure. Renew my strength, Father,
and let me draw comfort and courage from
Your promises and from Your unending love.
Amen

Notes:_____

_____

_____

_____

_____

_____

_____

_____

_____

_____

_____

_____

_____

_____

Day 9

Faith in God, Not in Oneself

Trust in the LORD with all your heart,
And lean not on your own understanding;
In all your ways acknowledge Him,
And He shall direct your paths.

Proverbs 3:5, 6

You do not have to be guilty of immorality to be subdued by the flesh. There are many people who are morally clean in their habits but who are full of self; these people must be seen, heard, satisfied, and gratified. They trust in themselves, and they forget their Creator.

When we are full of ourselves, we leave little room for God. Each day, therefore, we must fight the battle against self.

Who will you trust today? God or yourself? The answer, of course, should be obvious. You must trust God today and always.

For each of us, the time is surely coming when we shall have nothing but God. Health and wealth and friends and hiding places will all be swept away, and we shall have only God. To the man of pseudo faith this is a terrifying thought, but to a man of real faith, it is one of the most comforting thoughts the heart can entertain.

A. W. Tozer

He who is his own guide is guided by a fool.

C. H. Spurgeon

Never be afraid to trust an unknown future to a known God.

Corrie ten Boom

Do not be wise in your own eyes;
Fear the LORD and depart from evil.

Proverbs 3:7

A Prayer

Lord, when I trust in the things of this earth,
I will be disappointed. But, when I put my faith
in You, I am secure. In every aspect of my life,
Father, let me place my faith and my trust in
Your infinite wisdom and Your boundless grace.
Amen

Notes:_____

_____

_____

_____

_____

_____

_____

_____

_____

_____

_____

_____

_____

_____

Day 10

Faith in Adversity

Be of good courage,
And He shall strengthen your heart,
All you who hope in the LORD.

Psalm 31:24

Concentration camp survivor Corrie ten Boom relied on faith during her ten months of imprisonment and torture. Later, despite the fact that four of her family members had died in Nazi death camps, Corrie's faith was unshaken. She wrote, "There is no pit so deep that God's love is not deeper still." Christians take note: Genuine faith in God means faith in all circumstances, happy or sad, joyful or tragic.

We all must face the inevitable ups and downs of life, the triumphs and tragedies, the victories and defeats of this world. When the sun is shining and all is well, it's easy to have faith. But, when life takes an unexpected turn for the worse, as it will from time to time, your faith will be tested. In times of trouble and doubt, God remains faithful to you. Do the same for Him.

The way to Heaven is ascending;
we must be content to travel uphill,
though it be hard and tiresome, and contrary to
the natural bias of our flesh.
Jonathan Edwards

If we're going to stand up and make a difference
for Christ while others lounge about, you can
be sure we'll encounter hardships, obstacles,
nuisances, hassles, and inconveniences—much
more than the average couch potato.
And we shouldn't be surprised. Such difficulty
while serving Christ isn't necessarily suffering—
it's status quo.
Joni Eareckson Tada

Man's adversity is God's opportunity.
Matthew Henry

God is our refuge and strength,
A very present help in trouble.
Psalm 46:1

A Prayer

Dear Lord, sometimes this world is a difficult place.
When I am filled with uncertainty and doubt,
give me faith. In life's dark moments, help me
remember that You are always near and that You
can overcome any challenge. Today, Lord,
and forever, I will place my trust in You.
Amen

Notes:_____
_____
_____
_____
_____
_____
_____
_____
_____
_____
_____
_____
_____
_____

Day 11

Faith and Obedience

Jesus answered and said to him,
"If anyone loves Me, he will keep My word;
and My Father will love him, and We will come
to him and make Our home with him."

John 14:23 KJV

God has given us a guidebook for righteous living called the Holy Bible. It contains thorough instructions which, if followed, lead to fulfillment, righteousness and salvation. But, if we choose to ignore God's commandments, the results are as predictable as they are tragic.

Today—and every day after that—make yourself an example of righteous living. Walk with God and obey His teachings. When you do, you'll reap the blessings that God has promised to all those who live according to His will and His Word.

Absolute submission is not enough; we should go
on to joyful acquiescence to the will of God.

C. H. Spurgeon

Let us remember therefore this lesson:
That to worship our God sincerely we must
evermore begin by hearkening to His voice,
and by giving ear to what He commands us.
For if every man goes after his own way, we shall
wander. We may well run, but we shall never
be a whit nearer to the right way, but rather
farther away from it.

John Calvin

Therefore whoever hears these sayings of Mine,
and does them, I will liken him to a wise man
who built his house on the rock: and the rain
descended, the floods came, and the winds blew
and beat on that house; and it did not fall,
for it was founded on the rock.

Matthew 7:24, 25

A Prayer

Dear Heavenly Father, You have blessed me with
a love that is infinite and eternal. Let me
demonstrate my love for You by obeying Your
commandments. Make me a faithful servant,
Father, today and throughout eternity.
Let me show my love for You by sharing
Your message and Your love with others.
Amen

Notes:_____
_____
_____
_____
_____
_____
_____
_____
_____
_____
_____
_____
_____
_____

Day 12

Materialism: The Spiritual Roadblock

Therefore I say to you, do not worry about your
life, what you will eat or what you will drink;
nor about your body, what you will put on.
Is not life more than food and the body more
than clothing? Look at the birds of the air,
for they neither sow nor reap nor gather into
barns; yet your heavenly Father feeds them.
Are you not of more value than they?

Matthew 6:25, 26

We live in a materialistic world where too many people place their faith, not in God, but in things. Those who do so will be profoundly disappointed. On the grand stage of a well-lived life, material possessions should play a rather small role. Of course, we all need the basic necessities of life, but once we meet those needs for ourselves and for our families, the piling up of possessions creates more problems than it solves. Our real riches, of course, are not of this world. We are never really rich until we are rich in spirit.

Do you find yourself wrapped up in the concerns of the material world? If so, it's time to reorder your priorities by turning your thoughts and your prayers to more important matters. And, it's time to begin storing up riches that will endure throughout eternity: the spiritual kind.

Hold everything earthly with a loose hand,
but grasp eternal things with a deathlike grip.
C. H. Spurgeon

I have held many things in my hands, and
I have lost them all; but whatever I have placed
in God's hands, that I still possess.
Corrie ten Boom

Faith in God will not get for you everything
you want, but it will get for you what God wants
you to have. The unbeliever does not need
what he wants; the Christian should want
only what he needs.
Vance Havner

Do not love the world or the things in the world.
If anyone loves the world,
the love of the Father is not in him.
1 John 2:15

A Prayer

Lord, my greatest possession is my relationship with You through Jesus Christ. You have promised that when I first seek Your kingdom and Your righteousness, You will give me whatever I need. Let me trust You completely, Lord, for my needs, both material and spiritual, this day and always.
Amen

Notes:_____
_____
_____
_____
_____
_____
_____
_____
_____
_____
_____
_____
_____

Day 13

Sharing Your Faith

Also I say to you, whoever confesses Me before
men, him the Son of Man also will confess before
the angels of God. But he who denies Me before
men will be denied before the angels of God.

Luke 12:8, 9

Are you leaving tracks behind as you walk through this life? You most certainly are, but the question is this: Are they the right kind of tracks? It is not important how many homes you own, how much money you earn, how many trophies you receive, or how much work you accomplish. What *is* important is your relationship with your Savior *and* the way that you choose to live in response to His gift of salvation.

How many people are living godly lives because of your influence? How often have you shared your testimony? Are you an example of righteous living, of mountain-moving faith, and of total trust in God? If so, then you are leaving tracks that are worthy of your Savior. And those, dear friends, are the only tracks worth leaving.

Apostles are made from common men.
Mrs. Charles E. Cowman

I look upon all the world as my parish.
John Wesley

Father, make me a crisis man. Bring those
I contact to decision. Let me not be a milepost
on a single road; make me a fork, that men must
turn one way or another on facing Christ in me.
Jim Elliot

And as you go, preach, saying,
"The kingdom of heaven is at hand."
Matthew 10:7

A Prayer

Dear Lord, the life I live and the words
I speak bear testimony to my faith. Make me
a faithful servant of Your Son, and let my
testimony be worthy of You. Let my words
be sure and true, Lord, and let my actions
point others to You.
Amen

Notes:_____

_____

_____

_____

_____

_____

_____

_____

_____

_____

_____

_____

_____

_____

_____

Day 14

Faith in the Father

But now, O LORD, You are our Father;
We are the clay, and You our potter;
And all we are the work of Your hand.

Isaiah 64:8

Prayer is the most dynamic force available to any human being. Those who have learned to pray have learned to receive God's gifts, to live in the supernatural, and to be used by God to bless others. Those who have not learned to pray are still living on the natural level, and they find it impossible to accomplish the goals of life that Scripture sets forth.

The strength of your faith will be in direct proportion to the quality of your prayer life. So make yours a life of prayer. When you do, you'll be amazed at the things God has to say *to* you and the blessings He has in store *for* you.

The whole being of any Christian is Faith
and Love. Faith brings the man to God;
love brings him to men.

Martin Luther

Understanding is the reward of faith.
Therefore, seek not to understand that you may
believe, but believe that you may understand.

St. Augustine

Faith is like an empty, open hand stretched out
towards God, with nothing to offer
and everything to receive.

John Calvin

In You, O LORD, I put my trust;
Let me never be put to shame.

Psalm 71:1

A Prayer

Thank You, Dear Lord, for Your promises,
Your protection, Your faithfulness, and Your love.
Just as You have been faithful to me, Lord,
let me be faithful to You, today and every day.
Amen

Notes:_____

_____

_____

_____

_____

_____

_____

_____

_____

_____

_____

_____

Day 15

Faith Without Fear

Fear not, for I am with you;
Be not dismayed, for I am your God.
I will strengthen you, Yes, I will help you,
I will uphold you with My righteous right hand.

Isaiah 41:10

If God is for us, who can be against us? If God is for us, why should we be afraid of anyone? If God is for us, why should we be afraid of the unknown, the past, the future, the dark, or the doctors' reports? The answer, of course, is that when we have entrusted our lives to God, we have no need to fear anything.

If God was willing to give His Son for you, what in this world will He withhold from you if you trust Him and come to Him? Absolutely nothing. So be not afraid. You are God's child, and He will protect you today and forever.

When once we are assured that God is good,
then there can be nothing left to fear.
Hannah Whitall Smith

I pray that God will convince you of your security
in Christ. I pray that he will remind you that
your name is engraved on his hands. I pray that
you will hear him whisper, "So do not fear,
for I am with you" (Isaiah 41:10).
C. H. Spurgeon

Fear knocked at the door. Faith answered.
No one was there.
Anonymous

But He said to them, "It is I; do not be afraid."
John 6:20

A Prayer

Dear Lord, when I am fearful, keep me mindful
that You are my protector and my salvation.
Thank You, Father, for a perfect love
that casts out fear. Because of You,
I can live courageously and faithfully
this day and every day.
Amen

Notes:_____

_____

_____

_____

_____

_____

_____

_____

_____

_____

_____

_____

_____

_____

Day 16

Faith in Quiet Moments

Be still, and know that I am God.

Psalm 46:10

The Lord speaks in a still, small voice. When you are quiet before Him and seek His face, sometimes in the darkest moment, at the fourth watch of the night when there seems to be no hope and you are out on the waves, He will say, "Come." The best thing for you to do is to jump out of the boat instantly, and that is when you will walk on the water.

Is your faith being tested to the limits? Then perhaps you need to "tune out" the world and turn quietly to God. In the silence of your meditations, He is speaking to you. Listen, learn, and live accordingly.

The moment you wake up each morning,
all your wishes and hopes for the day rush at you
like wild animals. And the first job each morning
consists in shoving it all back; in listening to that
other voice, taking that other point of view,
letting that other, larger, stronger, quieter life
coming flowing in.

C. S. Lewis

When you meditate, imagine that Jesus Christ
in person is about to talk to you about the most
important thing in the world. Give him you
complete attention.

Fénelon

There is no work more likely to crowd out
the quiet hour than the very work that draws
its strength from the quiet hour.

Vance Havner

In quietness and confidence shall be your strength.

Isaiah 30:15

A Prayer

Dear Lord, in the quiet moments of this day,
I will turn my thoughts and prayers to You. In
these silent moments, I will sense Your presence,
and I will seek Your will for my life, knowing that
when I accept Your peace, I will be blessed
today and throughout eternity.
Amen

Notes:_____

_____

_____

_____

_____

_____

_____

_____

_____

_____

_____

_____

_____

_____

Day 17

Faith in
Our Salvation

For by grace you have been saved through faith,
and that not of yourselves; it is the gift of God,
not of works, lest anyone should boast.

Ephesians 2:8, 9

Saving faith brings us into the family of God. After salvation, we must look to the Lord for daily strength for the rest of our lives. We must look to the Lord in faith, in the midst of troubles and trials, for the provision of every need.

The familiar words of Ephesians 2:8 make God's promise perfectly clear: For by grace you have been saved through faith. We are saved not because of our good deeds but because of our faith in Christ. May we, who have been given so much, praise our Savior for the gift of salvation, and may we share the joyous news of our Master's love and His grace.

The way to be saved is not to delay,
but to come and take.

D. L. Moody

I now know the power of the risen Lord! He lives!
The dawn of Easter has broken in my own soul!
My night is gone!

Mrs. Charles E. Cowman

Amazing Grace! How sweet the sound
that saved a wretch like me! I once was lost
but now am found; was blind, but now I see.

John Newton

Truly my soul silently waits for God;
from Him comes my salvation.

Psalms 62:1

A Prayer

Dear Lord, I am only here on this earth for a brief
while. But, You have offered me the priceless gift
of eternal life through Your Son, Jesus. I accept
Your gift, Lord, with thanksgiving and praise.
Today and every day, let me share the Good News
of my salvation with all those who need
Your healing touch.
Amen

Notes:_____
_____
_____
_____
_____
_____
_____
_____
_____
_____
_____
_____
_____
_____
_____

Day 18

Faith Beyond the Crowd

And do not be conformed to this world,
but be transformed by the renewing of your mind,
that you may prove what is that good
and acceptable and perfect will of God.

Romans 12:2

God is looking for champions today who will run ahead of the crowd, who will not be embarrassed if they stumble and fall once in awhile, and who will not be afraid to have a few experiences that hurt their image and standing in society.

If you are going to run this race for God and make a mark on this generation, you must be willing to leap in, and if you lose your life in the doing, lose it for the glory of God! Remember: your goal must never be to please your neighbors, or anybody else for that matter. Your goal should be to please your Creator. And when you do so, you, dear friend, are not just a champion, you are God's champion.

A wise man may look ridiculous in
a company of fools.
Thomas Fuller

To know whom to avoid is a great means
of saving our souls.
St. Thomas Aquinas

Never be afraid of the world's censure;
it's praise is much more to be dreaded.
C. H. Spurgeon

Pure and undefiled religion before God
and the Father is this: to visit orphans
and widows in their trouble,
and to keep oneself unspotted from the world.
James 1:27

A Prayer

Dear Lord, direct my path far from the temptations
and distractions of this world, and make me
a champion of faith. Today I will honor You with
my thoughts, my actions, and my prayers.
I will worship You, Father, with thanksgiving
in my heart and praise on my lips,
this day and forever.
Amen

Notes:_____

_____

_____

_____

_____

_____

_____

_____

_____

_____

_____

_____

_____

_____

Day 19

Born Again Faith

Jesus answered and said to him,
"Most assuredly, I say to you, unless one is
born again, he cannot see the kingdom of God."

John 3:3

There is no way you can be in the will of God without being a born-again believer. It is my conviction that every life is a wasted life if it is lived without a personal experience which Jesus Christ called "the new birth."

God made man perfect in body, soul, and spirit. You may have a body and a soul; but if you do not have a human spirit indwelt by God's Spirit, if you are not a spiritual creature in a relationship with God, you are not complete and your life can never be in the will of God.

Have you been born again? This, dear friends, is the single, pivotal, most important question that you must answer while you dwell on this earth. And the answer to this question is yours and yours alone.

Jesus divided people—everyone—into two
classes—the once-born and the twice-born,
the unconverted and the converted.
No other distinction mattered.

E. Stanley Jones

The cross is not the terrible end to an otherwise
God-fearing and happy life, but it meets us at the
beginning of our communion with Christ. When
Christ calls a man, he bids him come and die.

Dietrich Bonhoeffer

The salvation of Jesus Christ enables
a man to see for the first time in his life.

Oswald Chambers

Just as Christ was raised from the dead by
the glory of the Father, even so we also
should walk in newness of life.

Romans 6:4

A Prayer

Lord, when I accepted Jesus as my personal savior,
You changed me forever and made me whole.
Let me share Your Son's message with my friends,
with my family, and with the world. You are
a God of love, redemption, conversion,
and salvation. I will praise you today and forever.
Amen

Notes:_____
_____
_____
_____
_____
_____
_____
_____
_____
_____
_____
_____
_____
_____
_____

Day 20

Have Faith . . . And Get Busy

But be doers of the word, and not hearers only,
deceiving yourselves.

James 1:22

Our faith must be an active faith. We must act upon our faith, or we risk losing it. Jesus taught His disciples that if they had faith, they could move mountains. You can too.

When you place your faith, your trust, indeed your life in the hands of Christ Jesus, you'll be amazed at the marvelous things He can do with you and through you. So strengthen your faith through praise, through worship, through Bible study, and through prayer. And trust God's plans. With Him, all things are possible, and He stands ready to open a world of possibilities to you if you have faith.

Pray as if it's all up to God, and
work as if it's all up to you.
Anonymous

Give to us clear vision that we may know where
to stand and what to stand for. Let us not be
content to wait and see what will happen,
but give us the determination to make
the right things happen.
Peter Marshall

Our faith grows by expression. If we want to keep
our faith, we must share it. We must act.
Billy Graham

Even so, every good tree bears good fruit,
but a bad tree bears bad fruit. A good tree cannot
bear bad fruit, nor can a bad tree bear good fruit.
Every tree that does not bear good fruit is
cut down and thrown into the fire.
Therefore by their fruits you will know them.
Matthew 7:17-20

A Prayer

Dear Lord, I have heard Your Word, and I have
felt Your presence in my heart; let me act
accordingly. Let my words and deeds serve as
a testimony to the changes You have made in
my life. Let me praise You, Father, by following in
the footsteps of Your Son, and let others
see Him through me.
Amen

Notes:_____

_____

_____

_____

_____

_____

_____

_____

_____

_____

_____

_____

_____

_____

Day 21

Faith Beyond Understanding

For now we see in a mirror, dimly,
but then face to face. Now I know in part,
but then I shall know just as I also am known.

1 Corinthians 13:12

There are times when God's ways and His leadings seemingly contradict common sense. Much of what God does is contrary to common sense, and that's as it should be. Man's "common sense" often leads him far from the safety of God's healing grace. But God's ways are always perfect.

Thank God for the sound mind He has given you, but in discerning the will of God for your life, don't lean too heavily upon your own mental horsepower. Instead of trusting your own intuition, trust God . . . prayerfully. Instead of relying on "common sense," rely on God's Holy Word. Instead of trusting yourself, trust your Savior. You, dear friend, may make mistakes, and lots of them. But God never has, and He never will.

God possesses infinite knowledge and awareness
which is uniquely His. At all times, even in the
midst of any type of suffering, I can realize that
He knows, loves, watches, understands,
and more than that, He has a purpose.

Billy Graham

God knows that we, with our limited vision,
don't even know that for which we should pray.
When we entrust our requests to him, we trust
him to honor our prayers with holy judgment.

Max Lucado

Walk by faith! Stop the plague of worry. Relax!
Learn to say, "Lord, this is Your battle."

Charles Swindoll

O LORD of hosts, Blessed is the man
who trusts in You!

Psalm 84:12

A Prayer

Dear God, sometimes this world can be a puzzling place, filled with uncertainty and doubt. When I am unsure of my next step, keep me mindful that You are always near and that You can overcome any challenge. Give me faith, Father, and let me remember always that with Your love and Your power, I can live courageously and faithfully today and every day.

Amen

Notes:_____

_____

_____

_____

_____

_____

_____

_____

_____

_____

_____

_____

_____

_____

_____

Day 22

Faith in the Dark

Fear not, for I have redeemed you;
I have called you by your name; You are Mine.

Isaiah 43:1

If you are a born-again believer who trusts God completely, rest assured. God will lead you to the place that is best for you, even if you cannot understand where He is leading you, or why. It is far better to step out "into the darkness" by trusting God than it is to step out "into man's light" and end up in despair and hopelessness.

Is God calling you to step out into the darkness? If so, answer His call. When you trust Him with all that you are and all that you possess, He will guide you. And if you are fearful, turn your fears over to the Father. He will never lead you astray, and He will protect you now, and throughout all eternity.

God alone can give us songs in the night.
C. H. Spurgeon

If a person fears God, he or she has no reason
to fear anything else. On the other hand,
if a person does not fear God, then fear
becomes a way of life.
Beth Moore

Do not build up obstacles in your imagination.
Difficulties must be studied and dealt with,
but they must not be magnified by fear.
Norman Vincent Peale

For God has not given us a spirit of fear,
but of power and of love and of a sound mind.
2 Timothy 1:7

A Prayer

Dear Lord, in the darkness of uncertainty,
give me faith. In those moments when I am afraid,
give me faith. When I am discouraged or confused,
strengthen my faith in You. You are the Good
Shepherd, let me trust in the perfection of
Your plan and in the salvation of Your Son,
this day and every day of my life.

Amen

Notes:_____

_____

_____

_____

_____

_____

_____

_____

_____

_____

_____

_____

_____

_____

Day 23

A Perfect Faith for Imperfect People

For all have sinned and fall short
of the glory of God.

Romans 3:23

Do not worry about what the critics, the agnostics, and the heathen infidels of our day say about you, your faith, or your Lord. God justified you. And if God says you are perfect in Christ, then you can be sure you are! You are not perfect in the flesh, but you are perfect in Christ.

Who will you try to please today: God or man? Your obligation is most certainly *not* to imperfect men or women. Your obligation is to an all-knowing and perfect God. Trust Him always. Love Him always. Praise Him always. And seek to please Him and only Him. Always.

Abide in Jesus, the sinless one—which means,
give up all of self and its life, and dwell in God's
will and rest in His strength. This is what brings
the power that does not commit sin.

Andrew Murray

We see how Jesus clearly chooses the way of
humility. He does not appear with great fanfare
as a powerful savior, announcing a new order.
On the contrary, he comes quietly,
with the many sinners who are receiving
a baptism of repentance.

Henri Nouwen

Sincere repentance is continual:
believers repent until their dying day.

C. H. Spurgeon

For sin shall not have dominion over you,
for you are not under law but under grace.

Romans 6:14

A Prayer

Dear Lord, today I will abide in Jesus. I will look
to Him as my Savior, and I will follow in His
footsteps. I will strive to please Him, and I will
separate myself from evils of this world. Thank
You, Lord, for Your Son. Today, I will count Him
as my dearest friend, and I will share His
transforming message with a world
in desperate need of His peace.
Amen

Notes:_____

_____

_____

_____

_____

_____

_____

_____

_____

_____

_____

_____

_____

_____

Day 24

Faith in God's Word

Your word is a lamp to my feet
and a light to my path.

Psalm 119:105

The Bible is as much the inerrant Word of God today as it was when God, by the Holy Spirit, had holy men of old write it word by word. As believers, we must study the Bible daily and meditate upon its meaning for our lives. Otherwise, we deprive ourselves of a priceless gift from our Creator.

God's Holy Word is, indeed, a transforming, life-changing, one-of-a-kind treasure. And, a passing acquaintance with the Good Book is insufficient for Christians who seek to obey God's Word and to understand His will.

Cling to the whole Bible, not to part of it. A man
is not going to do much with a broken sword.

D. L. Moody

I am a creature of a day. I am a spirit come from
God and returning to God. I want to know
one thing: the way to heaven. God himself has
condescended to teach me the way. He has
written it down in a book. Oh, give me that book!
At any price, give me the book of God. Let me
be a man of one book.

John Wesley

The vigor of our spiritual lives will be in exact
proportion to the place held by the Bible
in our lives and in our thoughts.

George Mueller

For the word of God is living and powerful, a
nd sharper than any two-edged sword, piercing
even to the division of soul and spirit, and
of joints and marrow, and is a discerner of
the thoughts and intents of the heart.

Hebrews 4:12

A Prayer

Dear Lord, the Bible is Your gift to me;
let me use it. When I stray from Your Holy Word,
Lord, I suffer. But, when I place Your Word
at the very center of my life, I am blessed.
Make me a faithful student of Your Word
so that I might be a faithful servant in Your world,
this day and every day.
Amen

Notes:_____

_____

_____

_____

_____

_____

_____

_____

_____

_____

_____

_____

_____

_____

Day 25

Faith in the Presence of God

Be strong and of good courage; do not be afraid,
nor be dismayed, for the LORD your God
is with you wherever you go.

Joshua 1:9 KJV

Every day when you begin the day, claim by faith the presence of God. Thank God and enjoy His presence every moment that you live. When we begin each day on our knees, in praise and worship to Him, God often seems very near indeed. But, if we ignore God's presence or—worse yet—rebel against it altogether, the world in which we live becomes a desolate spiritual wasteland.

In whatever condition you find yourself, wherever you are, whether you are happy or sad, victorious or vanquished, troubled or triumphant, celebrate God's presence. And be comforted. God is not just near. He is here.

God does not play hide-and-seek.
Erwin Lutzer

God is in the midst of whatever has happened,
is happening, and will happen.
Charles Swindoll

The core of all prayer is indeed listening,
obediently standing in the presence of God.
Henri Nouwen

The voice of the LORD is over the waters;
The God of glory thunders;
The LORD is over many waters
Psalm 29:3

A Prayer

Heavenly Father, help me to feel Your presence in every situation and every circumstance. You are with me, Lord, in times of celebration and in times of sorrow. You are with me when I am strong and when I am weak. You never leave my side, even when it seems to me that You are far away. Today and every day, God, let me feel You and acknowledge Your presence so that others, too, might know You through me.

Amen

Notes:_____

_____

_____

_____

_____

_____

_____

_____

_____

_____

_____

_____

_____

_____

_____

Day 26

Faith in Times of Prosperity

No one can serve two masters;
for either he will hate the one and love the other,
or else he will be loyal to the one and despise
the other. You cannot serve God and mammon.

Matthew 6:24

Sometimes our faith is tested more by prosperity than by adversity. Why? Because in times of plenty, we are tempted to stick out our chests and say, "I did that." But nothing could be further from the truth. All of our blessings start and end with God, and whatever "it" is, He did it. And He deserves the credit.

Who are the greatest among us? Are they the proud and the powerful? Hardly. The greatest among us are the humble servants who care less for their own glory and more for God's glory. If we seek greatness in God's eyes, we must forever praise God's good works, not our own.

Man's strength is more in God's way
than man's weakness.
C. H. Spurgeon

There is nothing so natural to man,
nothing so insidious and hidden from our sight,
nothing so difficult and dangerous, as pride.
Andrew Murray

God sends no one away empty except
those who are full of themselves.
D. L. Moody

Pride goes before destruction,
and a haughty spirit before a fall.
Better to be of a humble spirit with the lowly,
Than to divide the spoil with the proud.
Proverbs 16:18, 19

A Prayer

Heavenly Father, it is the nature of mankind to be prideful, and I am no exception, especially in times of prosperity. When I am tempted to be boastful, Lord, keep me mindful that all my gifts come from You. When I feel prideful, remind me that You sent Your Son to be a humble carpenter and that Jesus was ridiculed and crucified on a cross.
You are the Giver of all things good;
let me give all the glory to You. Always.
Amen

Notes:_____

_____

_____

_____

_____

_____

_____

_____

_____

_____

_____

_____

_____

_____

Day 27

Faith for a Loved One's Conversion

Be anxious for nothing, but in everything
by prayer and supplication, with thanksgiving,
let your requests be made known to God.

Philippians 4:6

Perhaps nothing hurts quite as badly as seeing someone you love reject the love of Jesus. When a loved one rejects God, the pain is twofold: Not only is he or she rejecting God's protection and comfort here on this earth, but the loved one is also rejecting eternal salvation, risking separation from you and from God forever.

Certainly you cannot force another person to accept Christ, but there are some things you can do:

• Live a victorious Christian life. As you concentrate on your own walk with the Lord, you provide a godly example: *"If some do not obey the word, they, without a word, may be won by the conduct of their wives, when they observe your chaste conduct accompanied by fear."* (1 Peter 3:1, 2).

• Pray earnestly. James 5:16 says, *"The effective, fervent prayer of a righteous man avails much."*

• Speak the truth as God opens the door. Preaching or nagging at your loved ones will do more harm than good, but when you have a natural opening in conversation and action, provide a loving witness.

• In your hearts sanctify Christ as Lord. *"Always be ready to give a defense to everyone who asks you a reason for the hope that is in you, with meekness and fear"* (1 Peter 3:15).

And finally, turn your concerns and your worries over to God and trust Him always. God's power to save is unlimited. Trust in Him for the salvation of those you love!

Praying for our children is a noble task. I
f what we are doing, in this fast-paced society,
is taking away from our prayer time for
our children, we're doing too much.
Max Lucado

By asking in Jesus' name, we're making
a request not only in His authority, but also
for His interests and His benefit.
Shirley Dobson

True prayer is measured by weight, not by length.
A single groan before God may have more
fullness of prayer in it than a fine oration
of great length.
C. H. Spurgeon

Therefore I say to you, whatever things you ask
when you pray, believe that you receive them,
and you will have them.
Mark 11:24

A Prayer

Dear Lord, today I pray for those who do not know Your Son. I pray they will open their hearts to Him and that they will receive His gift of salvation. And I pray for the courage to share my own testimony with those whom you place along my path, so that through my words and deeds, they, too, might come to know Jesus.

Amen

Notes:_____

_____

_____

_____

_____

_____

_____

_____

_____

_____

_____

_____

_____

_____

Day 28

Faith in the Promises of Jesus

For this cause I was born, and for this cause
I have come into the world,
that I should bear witness to the truth.

John 18:37

Jesus Christ is the cornerstone of the Christian faith. Either Jesus Christ is coequal with God the Father and God the Holy Spirit in all attributes pertaining to deity, or He is an absolute phony! He is not the god the cultists talk about. He is not only a great prophet, a good teacher, a wonderful example, and the Son of God; He is more. He is God the Son.

If Jesus were not God the Son, the Bible would be written about a mortal man who needed a Savior himself. He is, He was, and He ever shall be the Christ, the Son of the living God!

Dr. Jerry Falwell

Blessed assurance, Jesus is mine!
O what a foretaste of glory divine!
Fanny Crosby

The crucial question for each of us is this:
What do you think of Jesus, and do you yet
have a personal acquaintance with Him?
Hannah Whitall Smith

Jesus is not a strong man making men and
women who gather around Him weak.
He is the Strong creating the strong.
E. Stanley Jones

Then Jesus spoke to them again, saying,
"I am the light of the world.
He who follows Me shall not walk in darkness,
but have the light of life."
John 8:12

A Prayer

Dear Heavenly Father, I praise You and thank You for Your priceless gift: Jesus Christ. Let me share the Good News of the One who became a man so that I might become His, not only for today, but also for all eternity. Jesus is my Savior and my strength. I will welcome Him into my heart with love and thanksgiving, today and forever.

Amen

Notes:_____

_____

_____

_____

_____

_____

_____

_____

_____

_____

_____

_____

_____

_____

_____

_____

Day 29

Faith Beyond the Grave

Jesus answered and said to her,
"Whoever drinks of this water will thirst again,
but whoever drinks of the water that I shall give
him will never thirst. But the water that I shall
give him will become in him a fountain of water
springing up into everlasting life."

John 4:13, 14

For Christian believers, death is not an ending; it is a beginning. For Christian believers, the grave is not a final resting-place; it is a place of transition. Yet even when we know our loved ones are at peace with Christ, we still weep bitter tears, not so much for the departed, but instead for ourselves.

God promises that He is "near to those who have a broken heart" (Psalm 34:18). In times of intense sadness, we must turn to Him, and we must encourage our friends and family members to do likewise. Death can never claim those who have accepted Christ as their personal Savior. We have received the gift of life . . . abundant and eternal.

Death is an awful thing to those
who have their all in this world.
C. H. Spurgeon

Even life's happiest experiences last but
a moment, yet Heaven's joy is eternal. Some day
we will go to our eternal Home, and Christ will
be there to welcome us!
Billy Graham

One of these days, our Father will scoop us up
in His strong arms and we will hear Him say
those sweet and comforting words,
"Come on, child. We're going home."
Gloria Gaither

For the wages of sin is death, but the gift of God
is eternal life in Christ Jesus our Lord.
Romans 6:23

A Prayer

I know, Lord, that this world is not my home.
You have given me the priceless gift of eternal life
through Your Son Jesus. Keep the promise of
heaven fresh in my heart, and, while I am in this
world, help me to pass through it with faith in my
heart and praise on my lips . . . for You.
Amen

Notes:_____

_____

_____

_____

_____

_____

_____

_____

_____

_____

_____

_____

_____

_____

_____

Day 30

Faith in God

Blessed are all those who put their trust in Him.

Psalm 2:12

If only one sermon could be preached to all of God's people everywhere in the world, I believe it would have to be "Have Faith in God." Every life—including yours—is a series of successes and failures, celebrations and disappointments, joys and sorrows. Every step of the way, through every triumph and tragedy, God will stand by your side and strengthen you . . . if you have faith in Him.

Today, remember that God is always near and that He is your Protector *and* your Deliverer. Have faith in Him; He is your fortress. Trust Him always.

A mighty fortress is our God, a bulwark never failing. Our helper He, amid the flood of mortal ills prevailing. For still our ancient foe doth seek to work us woe His craft and power are great, armed with cruel hate, Our earth is not his equal.

Martin Luther

The Lord God of heaven and earth, the Almighty Creator of all things, He who holds the universe in His hand as though it were a very little thing, He is your Shepherd, and He has charged Himself with the care and keeping of you, as a shepherd is charged with the care and keeping of his sheep.

Hannah Whitall Smith

Cast your burden on the LORD,
And He shall sustain you;
He shall never permit the righteous to be moved.

Psalm 55:22

A Prayer

Dear Lord, Your love is eternal and Your laws are everlasting. When I obey Your commandments, I am blessed. Today, I invite You to reign over every corner of my heart. I will have faith in You, Father. I will sense Your presence; I will accept Your love; I will trust Your will; and I will praise You for the Savior of my life: Your Son Jesus.

Amen

Notes:_____

_____

_____

_____

_____

_____

_____

_____

_____

_____

_____

_____

_____

_____

Sunday Notes

Date:_____

Subject:_____

Key Scripture:_____

_____

_____

_____

_____

_____

_____

_____

_____

_____

_____

_____

_____

_____

_____

_____

_____

_____

_____

_____

_____

Notes

Date:_____

Subject:_____

Key Scripture:_____

_____

_____

_____

_____

_____

_____

_____

_____

_____

_____

_____

_____

_____

_____

_____

_____

_____

_____

_____

_____

_____

Notes

Date:_____

Subject:_____

Key Scripture:_____

_____

_____

_____

_____

_____

_____

_____

_____

_____

_____

_____

_____

_____

_____

_____

_____

_____

_____

_____

_____

_____

_____

_____

Notes

Date:_____

Subject:_____

Key Scripture:_____

_____

_____

_____

_____

_____

_____

_____

_____

_____

_____

_____

_____

_____

_____

_____

_____

_____

_____

_____

_____

_____

_____

Notes

Date:_____

Subject:_____

Key Scripture:_____

_____

_____

_____

_____

_____

_____

_____

_____

_____

_____

_____

_____

_____

_____

_____

_____

_____

_____

_____

_____

_____

_____

Notes

Selected Bible Verses

Have Faith in God

Now faith is the substance of things hoped for,
the evidence of things not seen.
Hebrews 11:1

Blessed are those who have not seen
and yet have believed.
John 20:29

Believe in the Lord your God,
and you shall be established.
2 Chronicles 20:20

But the just shall live by his faith.

Habakkuk 2:4

With Faith, We Can Move Mountains

For assuredly, I say to you, whoever says
to this mountain, "Be removed and be cast into
the sea," and does not doubt in his heart,
but believes that those things he says will be done,
he will have whatever he says.

Mark 11:23

Jesus said to him, "If you can believe, all things are
possible to him who believes."

Mark 9:23

You are the God who does wonders; You have
declared Your strength among the peoples.

Psalm 77:14

For with God nothing
will be impossible.

Luke 1:37

Have Faith, Not Fear

And immediately Jesus stretched out His hand
and caught him, and said to him,
"O you of little faith, why did you doubt?"
Matthew 14:31

Be not afraid; only believe.
Mark 5:36

In You, O LORD, I put my trust;
Let me never be put to shame.
Psalm 71:1

Cast your burden on the LORD,
And He shall sustain you;
He shall never permit
the righteous to be moved.

Psalm 55:22

Trust God Always

Trust in the LORD with all your heart,
and lean not on your own understanding;
In all your ways acknowledge Him,
and He shall direct your paths.
Proverbs 3:5, 6

It is better to trust in the LORD
Than to put confidence in man.
Psalm 118:8

These things I have spoken to you,
that in Me you may have peace.
In the world you will have tribulation;
but be of good cheer, I have overcome the world.
John 16:33

In God I have put my trust;
I will not fear.
What can flesh do to me?

Psalm 56:4

Trusting Our Savior

For the Son of Man has come
to save that which was lost.
Matthew 18:11

Then Jesus spoke to them again, saying,
"I am the light of the world.
He who follows Me shall not walk in darkness,
but have the light of life."
John 8:12

At the name of Jesus every knee should bow,
of those in heaven, and of those on earth,
and of those under the earth, and that
every tongue should confess that Jesus Christ
is Lord, to the glory of God the Father.
Philippians 2:10, 11

Most assuredly, I say to you,
he who hears My word and
believes in Him who sent Me
has everlasting life, and
shall not come into judgment,
but has passed from death into life.

John 5:24

My Favorite Bible Verses

_____

_____

_____

_____

_____

_____

_____

_____

_____

_____

_____

_____

_____

_____

_____

_____

_____

_____

_____

_____

_____

_____

_____

Additional